# DO YOU REALLY WANT TO MEET ANKYLOSAURUS?

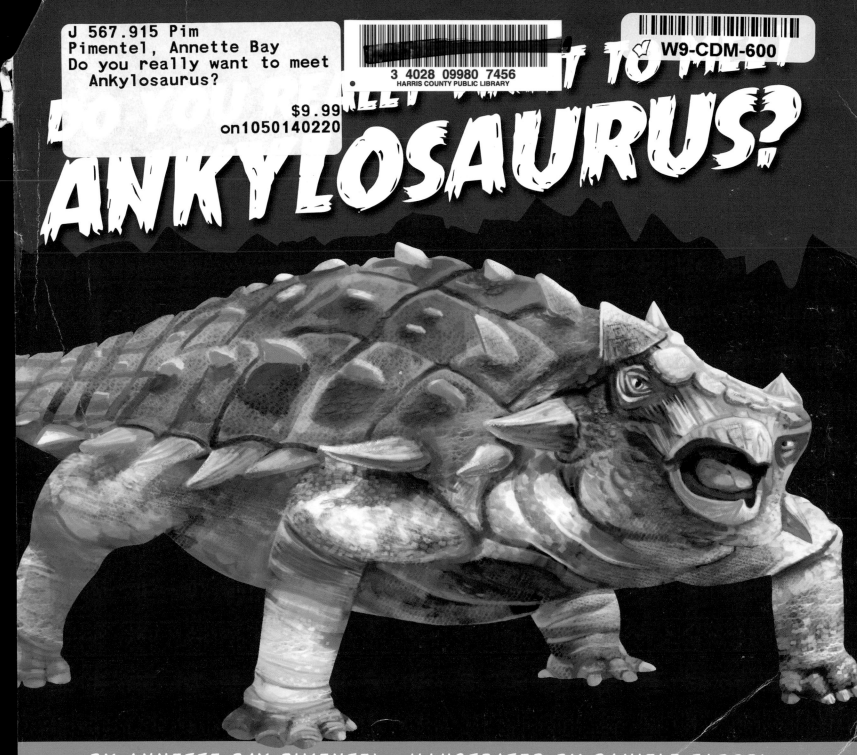

BY ANNETTE BAY PIMENTEL · ILLUSTRATED BY DANIELE FABBRI

AMICUS ILLUSTRATED and AMICUS INK
are published by Amicus
P.O. Box 1329, Mankato, MN 56002
www.amicuspublishing.us

EDITOR: Alissa Thielges
SET DESIGNER: Kathleen Petelinsek
BOOK DESIGNER: Veronica Scott

LIBRARY OF CONGRESS CATALOGING-IN-PUBLICATION DATA

Names: Pimentel, Annette Bay, author. | Fabbri, Daniele, 1978- illustrator.
Title: Do you really want to meet Ankylosaurus? / by Annette Bay Pimentel ; illustrated by Daniele Fabbri.
Description: Mankato, Minnesota : Amicus Illustrated and Amicus Ink, [2020] | Series: Do you really want to meet a dinosaur? | Audience: K to grade 3. | Includes bibliographical references.
Identifiers: LCCN 2018039669 (print) | LCCN 2018040767 (ebook) | ISBN 9781681517919 (pdf) | ISBN 9781681517094 (library binding) | ISBN 9781681524955 (pbk.)
Subjects: LCSH: Ankylosaurus--Juvenile literature. | Dinosaurs--Juvenile literature.
Classification: LCC QE862.O65 (ebook) | LCC QE862.O65 P556 2020 (print) | DDC 567.915--dc23
LC record available at https://lccn.loc.gov/2018039669

Printed in the United States of America
HC 10 9 8 7 6 5 4 3 2 1
PB 10 9 8 7 6 5 4 3 2 1

## ABOUT THE AUTHOR

Annette Bay Pimentel lives in Moscow, Idaho with her family. She doesn't have a time machine, so she researches the past at the library. She writes about what happened a long time ago in nonfiction picture books like *Mountain Chef* (2016, Charlesbridge). You can visit her online at www.annettebaypimentel.com.

## ABOUT THE ILLUSTRATOR

Daniele Fabbri was born in Ravenna, Italy, in 1978. He graduated from Istituto Europeo di Design in Milan, Italy, and started his career as a cartoon animator, storyboarder, and background designer for animated series. He has worked as a freelance illustrator since 2003, collaborating with advertising agencies and international publishers, including many books for Amicus.

Construction vehicles are built tough. An excavator can dig into hard ground. So could Ankylosaurus! It was a rugged digger, too. Don't you wish you could meet an Ankylosaurus?

First, you'll need a time machine because Ankylosaurus is extinct. Then travel back 66 million years to the Cretaceous Period. There were different types of ankylosaurs. To see the biggest kind, go to Montana.

You've landed in the river lowlands. Ankylosaurus might have lived high in the mountains. But it wandered here, too. You'll have to look hard, though. Scientists have found very few Ankylosaurus fossils. This dinosaur was rare!

Do you see the wide footprint with stubby toes?

Ankylosaurus could have made it. Follow the footprints.

No need to rush. Ankylosaurus walks very slowly.

You found an Ankylosaurus! Its back and sides are hard. Bony plates grow just under its skin. There's a big club at the end of its tail. That club hitting you would feel like a sledgehammer.

Ankylosaurus is 5 feet (1.5 m) wide and 20 feet (6.1 m) long. That's as long as a dump truck!

Ankylosaurus doesn't worry about manners. It chews off fern leaves. Its tongue shapes the mess into a gooey green ball. Slurp! Down goes the ball of fern.

Yikes! Ants! Ankylosaurus scoops out dirt with its beak. It digs up the ants and then gobbles them down. Sure, it's a plant-eater. But it eats tasty bugs when it can!

Ankylosaurus's nose is high on its head. Inside, its nasal passage twists every which way, like a crazy straw! Air in the nose cools down the blood. It also helps Ankylosaurus smell. And now it smells danger!

A T. rex! Blood rushes to Ankylosaurus's skin. It blushes slightly pink. That's a warning to the T. rex. Stay away! But this predator ignores the warning. It charges. Get out of the way—fast!

Ankylosaurus swings its tail. The club connects with T. rex's leg. Crunch! It breaks T. rex's ankle bone.

T. rex will not be chasing other dinosaurs for a while. It has learned not to mess with a grown-up Ankylosaurus.

Ankylosaurus will be safe. It may be slow, but it's tough. You, however, don't have a tail, let alone one with a club. You'd better hop back in the time machine. Goodbye for now, Ankylosaurus!

# WHERE HAVE ~~ANKYLOSAURUS~~ FOSSILS BEEN FOUND?

British Columbia

Alberta

Montana

Idaho

Wyoming

# GLOSSARY

**beak**—The horny edge of an animal's mouth, as in turtles, birds, and some types of dinosaurs.

**Cretaceous Period**—The time between 145.5 million and 65.5 million years ago. Dinosaurs lived during this time.

**extinct**—No longer found living anywhere in the world.

**nasal passage**—The tube that connects the nostrils with the lungs.

**predator**—An animal that hunts other animals for food.

**T. rex**—A meat-eating dinosaur of the Cretaceous Period.

# AUTHOR'S NOTE

Of course, time machines aren't real. But the details on Ankylosaurus in this book are from research by scientists who study fossils. Technology is used to make educated guesses on how dinosaurs looked and acted. In 2009, a study used a CT scan to calculate that an adult Ankylosaurus could swing its tail club hard enough to crush bone. New dinosaur discoveries are made every year. Look up the books and websites below to learn more.

## READ MORE

Clay, Kathryn. *Ankylosaurus and Other Armored Dinosaurs: The Need-to-Know Facts.* North Mankato, Minn.: Capstone Press, 2016.

Hansen, Grace. *Ankylosaurus.* Minneapolis: Abdo: 2018.

Sabelko, Rebecca. *Ankylosaurus.* Minneapolis: Bellwether Media, 2020.

## WEBSITES

NATIONAL GEOGRAPHIC KIDS: ANKYLOSAURUS
https://kids.nationalgeographic.com/animals/ankylosaurus/#ankylosaurus.jpg
Read more about this armored dinosaur.

PBS KIDS: DINOSAUR GAMES
https://pbskids.org/games/dinosaur/
Play games, watch videos, and try online activities to learn more about these fascinating extinct animals.

Every effort has been made to ensure that these websites are appropriate for children. However, because of the nature of the Internet, it is impossible to guarantee that these sites will remain active indefinitely or that their contents will not be altered.